James Mitchell

The Advice Savant

Volume I

Copyright 2007

Copyright 2007 by James Mitchell
All rights reserved
ISBN – 978-0-6151-8418-0

Dear Advice Savant,

About six months ago, a friend of mine moved in to the spare bedroom of my apartment. We've been friends for years, and it seemed like a great idea at the time, but now I think I'd really just rather live by myself. How can I ask my friend to leave, without sacrificing the friendship?

Ron – Portland, OR

Ron,

It's never easy asking a roommate to move out. There's a delicate balance required to maintain the friendship, while gently promoting an exit. The trick here is to get your roommate to *want* to move out. Some tips:

- Make the living situation, "unpleasant".
- Make the apartment somewhere they don't want to live.
- Turn the tone from "Get out", to "I'm really sorry you've decided to leave, but hey OK - see you later."

The idea is to be subtle. Slowly develop an atmosphere of unpleasantness that will gradually (almost subconsciously) drive your roommate to the conclusion that he'd really prefer to live somewhere else. But be subtle enough, so that he won't suspect you're doing anything on purpose, and therefore, won't be offended. Friend gone. Friendship preserved.

First off, start smoking. Ham. Right there in the apartment. There's nothing like a nice smoked ham, or hundreds of them; rapidly stacking up all around as you practice your new found love of curing meat. Your living room should literally have floor to ceiling hams. Make sure to further draw attention with well placed comments like "What should I eat with all these eggs?", "Boy, I could sure go for something salty.", and "What should we have for Easter this year?" Note: This tactic is especially effective if your roommate is a vegetarian. (Or - If somehow, he happens to be an actual pig.)

Start collecting something. Besides ham. No - not stamps or baseball cards either. Instead, consider something like fire alarms, fog horns (air horns), door bells or clown paintings. How about bags of human hair, or porcelain dolls (…with their sinister dead, lifeless eyes…)? Fill the bookcase with them! Your roommate will slowly begin to grow unsettled over time - sitting in your living room - surrounded by bags of hair - the gentle shriek of a fire alarm - and hundreds of vacant doll eyes staring him down.

Get a ventriloquist dummy. Always have it with you. It's there when you're watching television, eating dinner, or maybe going to the movies.

- Try to go for days, talking only through your dummy.
- Refer to it as "Our third roommate", and bring it out whenever family or friends stop by.
- Put the dummy's name on the mailbox. (Note: be sure to sign it up for lots of magazine subscriptions and junk mail.)

- Be sure to include the dummy in all conversations and especially important household decisions.
- Divide the utility bills in to three parts.

Make him an integral part of the circle. (How about having the dummy wake your roommate up in the morning?)

Get a pet - like an eagle. Give him a good name, like Freedom the eagle (as in freedom from your roommate). You'll probably need to clear some space on top of the bookcase, so it has a high place to perch. (Note: For a good nest to be possible, it's necessary to keep lots of loose sticks and branches lying around. Maybe some hay, or long grass.) Also be sure to stock the apartment with plenty of free roaming live rodents. Mice, some squirrels, maybe a snake or two. (Warning: When you see Freedom start to circle the room, its feeding time. Hit the dirt and cover your head, especially the eyes and ears.) Does your roommate already have a pet (a cat maybe)? Well not for long Ron…

Once again, be subtle. Small, almost unnoticeable changes to your behavior, and the environment, will slowly (and gently) push your roommate out of the apartment. Patience is the key here if you want the friendship to survive.

Dear Advice Savant,

I just finished college, and got my first "real" job as a computer software salesman. It's all very new to me, and I'm feeling pretty unsure of myself. Do you have any advice for someone just starting out in sales?

Ricky – Reno, NV

Ricky,

Congratulations on your new job! It must be exciting for you to get started on what's statistically sure to be a short lived, transitional, and unfulfilling job. Years from now, when you've finally ended up in a completely unrelated career, you can fondly look back on this first fumbling step in to the real world. Advice Ricky? Here's some: Don't go in to sales. Pick something else. Anything else really. A career in sales is awful. In fact, most "real" jobs are, but *especially* sales. Note: If you can, try to go back to school.

But whatever Ricky, congratulations.

If for some perverse reason you actually like the idea of sales, let's go through some basic points;
At the most fundamental level - To succeed in a sales position:
You'll need to always be thinking about *what you're selling* - and *who you're selling to*.

1. What am I providing?
2. How can I best identify who needs or wants it?

These are the two main questions you should be focused on immediately - right out of the gate. Stay centered on these core considerations, and you'll do fine.

Know what you're selling: I don't care what you're peddling, products, services, etc. In your case, it's software, but regardless, the rule stays the same. You need to know "it", inside and out. You're supposed to be the expert, and no one is going to take you seriously, let alone buy from you, if you convey the impression that you really don't know what you're talking about. Now, in your case (with software), it's (unfortunately) pretty difficult to understand the product completely. (Having the needed knowledge about drivers, hardware compatibility limitations, different PC operating systems, system bugs, etc. etc.) It's all extremely confusing, and incredibly boring.

If you were instead selling say, candles, it wouldn't be as tricky. *You light this end; and it burns- giving off heat, light and occasionally a pleasant odor.* But software is much more complex. My advice Ricky: Lie. Just make stuff up. Only the engineers really have any kind of handle on how software works, or what it can do. Most people buying software won't know the difference. Just practice inserting a few key phrases in to your sales dialogue. *Product Currently in Beta Testing...Diagnostic Parameters...Flux Capacitor...88mph...*, and so on. Just make sure to *sound* like you know what you're talking about.

Know your customers: The second key consideration. Who are you selling to? It's critical that you know your audience. Anyone in a sales position, who hasn't clearly identified their customer base, is destined to fail. Would you try to sell a hot dog to a vegetarian or diet pills to a sumo wrestler? How about a megaphone to a mime, or reality to George Bush? No Ricky, of course you wouldn't, because they aren't interested in buying it. Spend the extra time up front to really get to know your target customer. What do they need, or believe they need? What kinds of questions will they be asking you? BE READY! Know your customer. Or you'll have less success than Mel Gibson trying to sell a Wagner CD at the National Convention of Recovering Alcoholic Jewish Driving Instructors.

Post sale follow up, and customer service: Completely unimportant, and really not your problem Ricky. The last thing you want is to be hassled by customers, with questions about the software they just bought from you. It annoying and can ruin your sales "vibe". Instead, try to farm this annoyance out to a call center in India. It's easy, and usually pretty cheap. Also, remember that people have a short attention span, and an even shorter memory. Use this to your advantage. If a customer does happen to get you on the phone, just have some canned responses ready, and respond one of two general ways:

Deflection: It's someone else's fault or problem. This isn't my fault, try calling this other person.

Avoidance: Tell them that you'll get right back to them, and then forget all about it. Chances are they'll never call back. If they do, tell them you forwarded their issue on to someone else, and use the *Deflection* technique.

Dear Advice Savant,

I'm a small business owner. My company makes an all natural protein drink, made mostly from a combination of liquefied pork, chicken and beef. It's carbonated, comes in a soft drink style can, and sold in the beverage isle of grocery stores. We call it Carnesoft. Sales are slow, and only local. We make a modest but limited profit. How can I expand my sales, reach new markets, and increase profits?

Chuck – Bay City, TX

Chuck,

I think you're primed for success with your meat based cola. You just need that extra little push to elevate you into the big time.

First off (before anything else), you need a slogan - A catch phrase that will resonate in people's minds. It should be something simple and memorable that illustrates your product and stays in people minds:

- "Nature never had the *guts* to make this".
- "All the meat, none of the chewing". (Or simpler: "No-chew-meat".)
- "Pleased to meat you"!

Once you've got the catch phrase in place, start to think about your product line. What are you offering? What could you offer? Look at Diet or Cherry Coke. How can you expand on your core product line, and appeal to a larger market?
Some ideas:

- Carnesoft Extra Salty
- Gravysoft
- Butcher's Blend
- Carnesoft Rare

- A-1 Carnesoft
- Worcestersoft

So what's next? You've got a great product! How do you let people know? What makes them want to buy?

Marketing Chuck; Marketing.
The trick with Marketing is to go with what works. Tried and true techniques that won't just make people *want* Carnesoft, they'll *need* Carnesoft.

Professional Sports: Try to associate Carnesoft with professional sports, or celebrity athletes. Overdone? Sure, because it works. Try to play up the whole "protein energy drink" aspect of Carnesoft. It wouldn't hurt to add some pseudo-science, maybe something on the label talking about "vital mineral replacement" or "expedited enzyme restoration".

Hint: There's always a chiropractor out there somewhere who'll lend his name to add some medical credibility.

Pro athletes will do, or drink, whatever they think will make them faster, stronger or more resilient. They'll drink whatever will give them the "edge" they need to win. Think big here Chuck – Carnesoft on the sideline during the Super Bowl. Coaches yearning to have a victory cooler (heater?) of liquid meat poured over their head…

Cartoons: Try to tie in with a cartoon show or children's television series. These programs are marketing machines, and people have been using them for years to sell action figures and other toys. Why not a delicious and nutritious meat drink? Picture this Chuck: An updated version of Popeye, with a 21st century spin. Popeye's now a Navy Seal, who has a reputation for being a little "gristly". Spinach? – Gone. When Popeye needs his super strength to fight terrorists (Bluto), he drinks a can of Carnesoft. It's so perfect it's scary.

Scandal: There's no bad press Chuck, and there's no better way to get in the headlines than with a good scandal. You can do this a couple of ways; first would be to have a Carnesoft specific scandal. Maybe a rumor about the variety of meat that's *really* in Carnesoft (Human?), or the illegal process by which it's liquefied.

(Question: Chuck, how exactly *is* it liquefied?)

The second way to grab headlines is to involve Carnesoft with another scandal, preferable celebrity related. Example: "Paris Hilton enters rehab after accidentally drowning her dog Tinkerbell in bathtub of Carnesoft, during a drug crazed party."

Holidays: My last suggestion for you is to get Carnesoft associated with a holiday. Like eggnog at Christmas, or champagne on New Year's (Note: Thanksgiving - Turkey Carnesoft?), make people associate Carnesoft with a certain holiday every year. If possible, a religious holiday, as these come with a dedicated customer base, and will also give it more credibility. Easter wasn't always about candy Chuck, and St. Patrick 's Day wasn't always about green beer.

My recommendation: Work the Scientology angle. They're due for a recognized holiday, and this way, you can get in on the ground floor. A few years from now, people will be saying to each other "Happy Hubbard Day! Let's grab a Carnesoft and head over to the brain washing center for a personality test.

Dear Advice Savant,

I have a real problem with strangers talking to me on flights. They always seem to start these long conversations. I don't want to seem rude, so I just sit there and smile, waiting for the flight to be over. Next week, I fly to Australia. The flight is like 30 hours long, and I just know I'll get stuck sitting next to a talker. What can I do?

Orville – Arlington, TX

Orville,

A lot of us out here, including myself, feel your pain. Listening to a long, drawn out story about someone's grandchildren, or a dissertation on a plan to renovate the kitchen, can be torture.

This is for you talkers out there: We may be forced to sit uncomfortably close together, but please don't make it worse by talking. We don't care about your favorite sports team, your car, political views or prostrate problems. Leave it on the ground.

Orville, there are ways to avoid the talker. Here are a few ideas that will make you flight much easier:

Plan ahead: Start planning early. Eat plenty of garlic and onions for several days leading up to the flight. No clean clothes. No showers. In fact, run to the gate at the airport, so you'll have a fresh coat of sweat on you when you sit down. It wouldn't hurt to comment on this either; "Boy, I sure am sweaty! Hope I remembered deodorant!" (Note: Do not remember deodorant.)

Apparel: I would recommend one of those color changing shirts from the 80s. (Reminder: Put your hand on the sleeve, and it changes color.) In addition to being cool and attractive, this shirt serves a purpose. Before the plane even takes off, as soon as you sit down, start asking the talker to touch you. "If you touch me, I turn colors." Become insistent if needed; "Touch my shirt!" Keep asking. If they do touch your shirt, scream and giggle uncontrollably - stand up and show everyone else seated around you. "They touched me! I changed colors!"

At this point, you probably don't have to worry about anyone talking to you for the rest of the flight. But, just to make sure...

Pretend to fly the plane: Try to get some of those little wings the pilots wear on their shirt. (Note: The flight attendants usually only give these out to kids, but if you ask nicely or slip them a few bucks, you can get some.) Put on the wings, and begin to work the controls. Flip imaginary switches, push invisible buttons. Look like you know what you're doing. Use the "stick" (Rolled up magazine?), to taxi down the runway and take off. Whoa! - Orville, don't forget those flaps! Feel free to play the role of both pilot and co-pilot during takeoff. Make sure they talk to each other! Use your complimentary headphones to radio the tower, and include lots of airline lingo like "roger", "check" and "three-niner".

After you're airborne, take off the headphones, turn to the would-be talker and say in a very steady and serious voice: "I know that seemed complicated and scary, but trust me; it's still the safest way to travel. Would you like some wings?"

At mealtime: Be sure to wear your lobster bib and insist on using chopsticks - regardless of what's being served. Ask the talker if they would please blow on your food for you; as it's too hot, and you don't want to burn your mouth.

Backup plan: At this point Orville, you can be almost guaranteed a quiet flight. However, if your neighbor does decide to talk with you, remain calm. As soon as they start talking, try to look concerned. Furrow your brow, and look to the side as if you're concentrating. After a few minutes, ask if they have an extra diaper.

Good luck Orville! Have a great flight!

Dear Advice Savant,

I'm supposed to run the Twin Cities Marathon in a couple of weeks. I'm not a natural athlete, and I haven't been training at all. There's no way I can run 26 miles. To make things worse, everyone at the office knows I've signed up. If I don't, I'll never live it down. What do I do?

Elsie – St. Paul, MN

Elsie,

You're in a bit of a bind. But don't worry; we'll get you through this.

You say "Sure", "I'll sign up for the marathon, that's months away." And before you know it, those months have become weeks, days, or even hours. It's a common problem, happens to people all the time. What do you do? If I may Elsie, a few thoughts;

First off, whether you actually end up running this thing or not, you want to set the right tone at work. As far as they're concerned you have every intention of running. *Become* that runner Elsie. Wear a headband at all times, a big one.

- Sprint everywhere you go around the office.
- Dump glasses of water on your head.
- When meeting with colleges, kick your leg up on the table and do that touch your foot stretch thing.
- In the elevator (yes, you can still take the elevator) jog in place and check your pulse. (For the record, no, I don't know how to check a pulse either. But, if you hold your wrist, and look at your watch, people will think you do.)

Fake it Elsie. Sell it Elsie. *Be* that runner.

Now, let's assume for a minute that you're still going to try and *run* the race. There are a few options on how you might actually pull it off;

1. Steroids. Yes, steroids. It's not like you're competing in the Olympics or anything here. All eyes aren't on you. There's no world record at stake, and you won't end up on a cereal box. It's not even like you're trying to win, you just want to finish. So, unless you work in a lab or something, no one is going to test you - or even care for that matter. Get off your moral high horse and dope up.
2. This second option is based on the power of motivation. (I'm a little hesitant to recommend it, as it could be dangerous.) The properly motivated human mind is a powerful thing. You'll have to ask yourself how important running this race is to you. I can't really go in to the details, I will simply say this:

   Starting Line = Poison

   Finish Line = Antidote
3. Use physics. Science tells us that an object in motion will stay in motion until a force acts to stop it. The force acting to

slow an object, must overcome the force keeping it in motion, mass and momentum, etc. Start eating Elsie. Get as big, or as *massy* as you can. The idea here is to get you, and your mass, in motion - then let the science take over. If my (untested) theory is correct (and they always are), once we get you moving, the momentum should carry you all the way. We just need to get you massy enough to counteract Earth's gravity for 26 miles (think: low orbit). There are a few details that I will trust you to work through (getting you started, stopping you, turning, etc). I'm sure you'll figure it out. Get you mass moving Elsie!

Now I know what you're saying, "Advice Savant, I just don't think I can run. What now?" Well, if you're really sure you can't possibly run the race Elsie, we have options here too.

1. Be at the finish line on race day. No hurry, just make sure to be there when the *slower* finishers start coming in. People who've made it, but just barely. People who are dehydrated, starving, exhausted, and completely out of it. People easily lured behind a tree or car with a bottle of water, or maybe a granola bar. People who are easily overpowered, because they're already half unconscious. People who've just given you their "Twin Cities Marathon Finisher" t-shirt and

medallion, which you'll wear proudly to the office the next day.

2. Break your leg. Or, have someone else do it (although that leaves a witness). Fall off your bike, jump in front of a car, find a columnist with a bat, throw yourself down the stairs, or whatever works for you. Painful? You bet Elsie. But so is living in ridicule and shame. Breaking your leg means that you'll get co-worker sympathy, not grief, for skipping the race.

Good luck Elsie!

Dear Advice Savant,

My wife and I were at a "friends" wedding the other day. It was awful. The ceremony, which lasted over 3 hours, was held in what was basically a trailer park outside of Reno. The vows, when the couple could remember them, were cold and rehearsed. The music (Duran Duran – The Wedding Album) was played through the car stereo of a monster truck, parked behind the "alter" (stack of wooden shipping pallets). It was terrible. Yet, as we all gathered around the barrel fire during the reception to roast our hot dogs on sticks; my wife and I talked non-stop about how "creative" and "lovely" the service was. We didn't even think twice, just lied through our teeth (not everyone there had teeth). My question is this; when is it socially and morally acceptable to lie?

Derrick – Las Vegas, NV

Derrick,

You've hit on something here that's hard for me to answer. Yes lying is wrong. Most people will agree on this. But there are two conditions that question this thinking:

1. When a lie is told to avoid hurting someone – i.e. doing something wrong, with the intent of doing something right. What makes a lie wrong? The action or the intent?
2. When you're pretty sure you won't get caught, or even if you do, no one will actually do anything about it.

I'm afraid I can't put this in black and white for you Derrick. There's no rule, or formula here to follow. It just has to come down to the situation, and your gut and personal moral feeling on what's right. What I can do though is give you a few examples to consider.

Lying to Family

Situation 1: Your great aunt has just given you a sweater for Christmas, its bright orange, with bells, feathers and ribbons on it. On the front, a smarmy picture of Bill O'Reilly (sneering) is

stitched on with sequins and rhinestones. Several small stuffed birds attach to the sleeve with Velcro.
Acceptable lie: "I love it. I'll wear it all the time. And I'll wash it in the –No Spin- cycle."
Note: This applies to gifts from anyone in the family.

Situation 2: Your brother is having the entire family over for a special dinner, maybe even Thanksgiving. He's not a good cook (on the way home you'll need to swing by the poison control center at the ER, hoping to avoid several days in the bathroom).
Acceptable lie: "That was delicious. You should really cook more often."
Note: This would also apply to dinner with other family members, parents, etc. - ESPECIALLY dinner with your wife.

Situation 3: Your daughter is playing a "pine cone" in the elementary school play. She forgets her lines, misses all of her queues, and in a freak miscommunication - accidentally lights one of the stage props on fire, setting of the sprinklers, and causing everyone the flee the auditorium.
Acceptable lie: "You did great sweetheart. I can't wait to see your next play!"

Note: This would also apply to children's sporting events, choir/band performances, "magic" shows, or artwork of any kind.

Lying to Friends

Situation 1: You're visiting s friend's new house for the first time. The outside resembles a WWII bunker, complete with mortar holes in the yard. The inside is adorned with bean bag chairs, tiger print wallpaper, and a coffee table made out of empty beer cases. Chuck Norris posters and a confederate flag are hung on the walls.
Acceptable lie: "I really like what you've done with this place. It's very "homey."
Note: Get a new friend. Seriously, this guy sounds like a nut job.

Situation 2: Your friend has just broken it off with his girlfriend of 3 years. She had a great sense of humor, got along with everyone, had a master's degree, did volunteer work, and was beautiful.
Acceptable lie: "You'll totally find someone better."
Note: Don't lie too much or be too critical of an ex, because they sometimes get back together.

Lying to the Country

Situation: You *really* want to invade a country and dispose a dictator that poses no real threat to national security. But you need public backing. Due to lucky happenstance, your country has recently gone through a national tragedy, is angry and scared, and less likely to challenge what would otherwise be a *highly* questionable decision.
Acceptable lie: "We know he's been absolutely devoted to trying to acquire nuclear weapons, and we believe he has, in fact, reconstituted nuclear weapons."
Note: This is fine, but DO NOT - lie about extra marital affairs.

Invading other nations; causing the death of thousands of American troops and countless civilians; damaging the integrity and reputation of the country; becoming a recruitment poster child for terrorist organizations - all acceptable under the higher moral justification.

Cheating on your wife, that's different. Remember, it's the higher principles that matter when lying. Invading a country can be excused, and the lies ignored. But being unfaithful? That could result in public inquiries, morel condemnation, and millions of tax dollars spent to investigate and prosecute.

Derrick, as you're weighing your lies, make sure to remember what's important. It will guide your decisions, and help you make the right choice.

Dear Advice Savant,

Last month I quit my job as an engineer, to pursue my dream of becoming a magician. So far, not much has happened. I guess I really don't know how to get started. Being an engineer is all I've ever done. Do you have any advice for someone looking to change their life? Start a new profession?

Melvin – Boston, MA

Hello Melvin,

I just want to mention something quickly here; Magicians are not actually magic. They're just regular people who perform tricks. You probably already know this, but I just wanted to make sure. You're an engineer, and I'm guessing probably a geek, into sci-fi, fantasy dragons and everything. I just want you to be clear; you won't actually become *magic*. You can't actually become your on-line World of Weirdcraft alter-ego.

Also Melvin, know what you're getting in to. This really isn't just a career change we're talking about; it's more of a lifestyle change. You're becoming an entertainer. You'll be working odd hours, taking whatever "gigs" you can get, often in strange or scary places. This won't be the exciting and romantic fantasy life you're envisioning. Also, magicians are WAY down at the bottom of the list when it comes to respect in the entertainment world. They're in the same category as mimes, strippers, Rosie and Carrot Top.

Even the best and most famous magicians in the world, are still seen as kind of "odd". Sure, they're fun to watch (from a distance), but you really don't want to sit next to them on a bus, or get trapped in an elevator with them.

However, as long as you're clear on what this means Melvin, here's some advice on what to do next:

Learn the Trade

There are a million books you can buy, lessons you can take or videos you can watch. But if you really want to learn how to be a true magician, you'll need to get some hands on experience. Become a master's apprentice.

1. Find a magician, who's willing to teach you, or needs an assistant.
2. Spend 20 years as an apprentice.
3. You're ready. Steal all of their tricks, and escape.

Manage Your Career as a Business

You're en entertainer now, but you still need to make money. Think of yourself as a one magician business. Make sure to consider profit and loss, expenses, marketing, etc.
Example: Billy Nelson's 6th birthday party. Make sure to balance the revenue gained (your fee), against the expenses: magic trick supplies, rabbit food, gas money, etc.

Note: If the Nelson's "forget to pay", don't be shy about making something "disappear" on your way out the door, (like jewelry or silverware) to help your business stay profitable.

Also, make sure to take advantage of all your tax benefits. The Nelson's silverware, jewelry, or cash payments are hard for the government to track. Make sure to refuse any credit card payments. Keep things off the books. Try to use a fake name at the pawn shop, and keep a low profile. Don't be to "flashy" with your money. When you do pay taxes, make sure to take advantage of all your write-offs (cape dry cleaning, wand tuning, rabbit breeder, etc.)

Insurance is very important:

- Carry plenty of dismemberment insurance, in case that whole "sawing the lady in half" thing goes awry.
- Carpal Tunnel Syndrome is common among those who perform card tricks; make sure your medical needs are covered.
- Most general plans don't cover Magic Dust Lung. If untreated, this can be fatal, so be wary.

Find Your Niche

Lastly, try to find something to help you stand out. Do something unique that will get you noticed. These days, everyone is spending time underwater or frozen in a block of ice. Some magicians even roam the streets performing for people, so they can film it and show it on TV later. (Note: this is a new type of magic called "Video Editing".) Find something that no one else does Melvin. Make it seem cool and dangerous. If it's illegal, do it in another country. And never forget the "magic" of good PR.

One last thing Melvin; if you do get frozen in ice, try to stay there. Leave a note or something with instructions to thaw you out in a few hundred years. You're a sci-fi geek right? The future might be cool.

Good luck Melvin!

Dear Readers,

Every week, I get thousands of letters and e-mails from good people like you, who just need some advice. I try to answer as many as I can, but as you can imagine, it's impossible. Deciding which questions to answer, which people to help, is an ongoing challenge for me. How to you put one person's problems above another? How do you decide who gets a reply, and who doesn't? Everyone needs good advice from time to time. Everyone deserves help; except these people. Here are some questions that didn't even make my short list.

Some people simply deserve to suffer.

Dear Advice Savant,

I'm super attractive, and really rich. I had to quite modeling to manage my inheritance fund full time. Whenever I go out to a bar or restaurant, I'm mobbed by women. Last week I was chased down by a crazed waitress who kept trying to tear my silk shirt off. I barely managed to make it to my Porsche and escape. It's so annoying. I'm starting to get depressed! I've hardly left my yacht all week. Do you know how redundant parties can get on a yacht? I'm about ready to take my private jet and fly to my private island, just for a change of scenery. What can I do? How can I make myself more "manageably" attractive?

Chaz – Miami, FL

Dear Advice Savant,

I have a show on the Fox "news" channel. Lately, my ratings have been falling, fast, and I have no idea why. I've been using all the usual tactics to boost my appeal, but nothing seems to work. I've tried to leverage 9/11, playing off fear and patriotism. I make daily references to the leftist democrats and their secular, communist, tax raising, homosexual marriage pushing, socialist loving, America hating ways. I bully guests on my show, claim to be impartial, while constantly reminding everyone how traditional I am. I push my belief in traditional American values, and traditions.

Traditions. American traditions. God fearing, apple pie eating, war winning, traditions. But nothing works. My ratings keep dropping, and I'm worried that soon I'll need to compete with real journalists or go back to hosting A Current Affair! What do I do?
Bill – New York, NY

Dear Advice Savant,
People keep trying to stick stuff to the back of my neck. Post-it notes, tape, scratch and sniff stickers, you name it. I haven't caught any of them in the act yet, but I can tell. On the bus, in line at the grocery store, everywhere I go. I can't wear a turtleneck every day! What do I do? How can I keep people from sticking stuff to the back of my neck?
Ed – Minneapolis, MN

(None of these will ever get a response.)

Dear Advice Savant,

Last Sunday, I woke up to find a 600 pound bear in bed next to me. Naturally, I panicked, screamed, and ran out of the house. From my neighbor's house I called 911, all I could hear was growling, crashing noises and breaking glass. By the time animal services arrived, the bear had destroyed almost everything I owned. The house was ruined. I guess I'm lucky to be alive, but I just don't see how something like this can happen. How does a bear end up in your bed? What are you supposed to do if you find one?

Carla – Newark, NJ

Wow Carla,

I'm really not sure what to say about this. So let me just fire off a few…

- Must have been some night at the bar (or zoo?).
- Not sure, but you might want to pay off that debt to the Mafia.
- Why do you always feel the need to "one up" Jane Goodall?
- Did he answer to Grossman? Because this may explain why they keep losing games.
- That's pretty em-bear-assing Carla.
- Sounds like you bear-ly got out of there.

Seriously though Carla, bear with me a moment. This kind of question isn't as strange as you might think. Granted, it usually comes from campers…sometimes zookeepers…bees…but whatever. Unless you're a bearded man living in the mountains who likes to hang out with Uncle Jessie and his donkey; this is not the way you want to wake up. (Especially on a Sunday, when you'd rather sleep in and maybe read the paper, except those bears always take the paper in to the bathroom with them, and you really don't even want it when their done with it believe me…)

Anyway Carla, let's talk about how this might happen.

Food

Bears are always going to look for food, whether it's in the woods, or in your house. This is the number one reason bears will come. (Except for bear pheromones during mating season; but if that's what's going on Carla, you need far more help than I can provide. You're a freak.)

Here are a few tips on food safety:

- Don't eat food in bed. Especially berries and salmon.
- Try not to leave food lying around your house. (Note: Cub Scouts and Pets are food to a bear.)
- Even though it's cool and trendy, a bee hive in the living room is a magnet for honey starved bears.
- Find an excuse to avoid taking care of your brothers bear cub while he's out of town. (Not food related, but important.)
- While it may be cheap and effective, avoid using gravy as a fabric softener when washing sheets, pajamas and underwear.
- Be sure to package any blood or goat parts in Tupperware (and put it in the fridge), immediately after your cult ceremony is over.

If you can eliminate the food issue Carla, you're pretty much guaranteed not to have a bear wander in to your house, let along your bed.

But what if it does? What to do then? How do you deal with it?

Bears are like people. Different bears have different temperaments, and personalities. Some are aggressive, some are docile. Some are smart, some are stupid. The key to successfully handling a bear encounter is to know what you're up against.

A few key examples:

- Black Bear: Very common bear, and not very aggressive. This type of bear can usually be scared off by yelling, banging some pots together or playing one of Paris Hilton's songs.
- Brown Bear: More aggressive (this family includes the Grizzly and Kodiak bear families). If you find this bear in your house, point behind it and yell "pic-i-nik basket!" While it's distracted, dive out the nearest window, and run like Boo Boo.

- Bear Emanilow: While it won't kill you, this type of bear can cause years of pain and emotional distress. If confronted, keep calm. Wait for the bear to get distracted, perhaps looking in a mirror, then hit it with several tranquilizer darts and call the authorities.
- Marion Bear(e): Very dangerous. This variety of bear is mild mannered, almost congenial. But still a bear. The reason this bear is so scary, is its immunity to most tranquilizer darts. This variety of bear spends most of its life, taking drugs *on purpose*, making it immune to normal defensive sedatives. If confronted, keep calm. Try to keep the bear in good spirits (a compliment to the bear wouldn't hurt). When the bear borrows your pocket mirror and leaves to use the bathroom, run like Boo Boo.
- Bear Ebonds: See above.
- Dave Bear(e): A smart bear. This bear is "ten pounds of clever in a five pound bag." While normally harmless, avoid critique of this bears fiction work as this may upset or offend the bear.

Good luck Carla!

Dear Advice Savant,

I have a cat that misbehaves. If dinner is late, she meows incessantly until fed. If I'm away to long, I come home to find clawed-up furniture, or my shoes turned in to a litter box. It's as if my cat thinks she owns the place! Almost like I'm the pet! What can I do? How do I take back control of my own house from my cat?

Matilda – Hayward, WI

Matilda, you're not alone.

There are lots of cat owners out there who have similar problems. It's sad really. Cats are (to put it simply) evil, wretched beasts. Clever – lazy – selfish – sneaky - egocentric and rude little animals (on a good day). Matilda, if it wasn't for the daily food you provide, your cat would be happy not having you around at all. She'd be perfectly content playing with her beam of sunlight, or imaginary "thing" in the corner. Cats are bad news Matilda. I'd like to offer the following advice: Get a dog.
But unfortunately, we're obviously past that point. So Matilda, unless you're willing to consider a donation to medical science (*do it*), we'll need to deal with the issue at hand: Controlling the cat you already have.

The key here is to re-establish your dominance in the relationship. You need to re-assert your authority. But how you ask? Simple: Leverage Evolution.

The common (tiny, harmless) house cat is closely related (genetically) to the lion, the tiger, the cheetah, etc. Some of the most fearsome, majestic and awesome animals in nature are distant

relatives of your house cat. An evolutionary relationship which (while probably contributing to her enormous kitty ego), can be used to your advantage Matilda.
Start off with a casual walk around the block (or "neighborhood safari"). This will get your cats genetic juices flowing. I'm not sure exactly what kind of local wildlife you have in Wisconsin Matilda, but if possible during your stroll, try to stalk and kill an antelope or zebra. (Hint: If found in a herd, weed out the sick and/or weak. They're slower, and easier to catch on foot.) If you can't find a "safari quality" kill, any poodle will do (Note: not a *real* dog).

Here's the important part though Matilda: Whatever you end up killing, make sure *you eat first.*

"Eating priority" is what you want Matilda. When a bunch of lions take down a prey, the leaders get to eat first. This establishes a pecking order. This is the law of nature, the way of the predatory animals, and something your house cat will respect. You are the leader – You are in charge!

Make sure you eat your fill of the carcass *before* allowing your cat to eat (let it watch you pick the poodle fur from your teeth). This will establish your dominance and authority. Your cat will understand this, and respect you as its master. (Note: Maintain this hierarchy in all other ways i.e. balls of yarn, the scratching post, sun beams, the litter box, etc.)

Regain your pride Matilda! No pun intended.

One other quick thing: If you can't see yourself stalking prey around the neighborhood, consider using catnip. Drugs are always effective, and once your cat is hooked, you've got her. She'll do anything for her next fix, and fall in line quickly. Just make sure there aren't any other dealers nearby.

Remember – The first ones free.
Good luck Matilda!

Dear Advice Savant,

I'm the president of the Atlanta chapter Scott Baio fan club. We meet once a week and talk about Scott, watch his movies and TV shows, that kind of thing. I really enjoy it. Next month, the national convention is being held here in Atlanta, and because I'm the local president, I'm in charge of coordinating the entire event! This is the national Scott Baio fan club we're talking about – there could be literally millions of people there! I've never done anything like this before, what do I do?

Ellen – Atlanta, GA

Keep it together Ellen!

Remember, you're doing this for Scott Baio! You'll do fine.

Planning a large event (millions of people? really?) like this can seem like a daunting task. But it's really just a matter of careful planning and organization. Don't let yourself get too worried about all the little details; food, rest room facilities, security considerations, etc. Stay focused on what's important – Scott Baio. Everyone's there for the same reason: Love and respect for a great actor and the incredible work he's done over the years. If you plan with this in mind, all the other little details will work themselves out. Give the people what they want Ellen.

Here a rough suggestion on how you might want to plan the day's events. Just to get you started:

8:00 – 9:00: Welcome reception. Guests are greeted and given "name bandana's" (worn around the leg, just above the knee) in favor of the standard name tag. Attendees will be free to mingle and meet one another. Coffee, bagels and doughnuts are served.

9:00 – 10:15: First session of round table discussions. Guests will be free to attend their choice of open forums:

- *Happy Days*: Discussion of the relationship between Fonzie and Chachi. Key questions: Was Fonzie jealous of Chachi's "cool"?
- Ethics Debate: Is it OK to name your pets Joanie and Chachi, if they don't love each other?
- *Battle of the Network Stars*: In 1981 Scott Baio was the ABC team captain – was he the greatest team captain ever? Of any sports team? Ever?

10:30 – 11:45: Second session of round table discussions.

- *Charles in Charge*: Could the way Charles looked after the Powell family children be considered the new standard in modern parenting? What can we learn from his example? Should this television show be incorporated as a learning tool for day care providers and teachers?
- If Chachi had jumped the shark instead of Fonzie, would *Happy Days* still be in production?
- 2004 – Scott plays Stan Bobbins in *Super Babies: Baby Geniuses 2*. What the %@&#?

12:00 – 1:30: Lunch

1:45 – 3:30: Viewing of Scott Baio playing Barney Springboro in 1982's feature film *Zapped.*

3:30 – 4:15: Brief review of the film, and lecture covering its impact on modern culture and art given by Dr. Ringo Koop, Professor of Celebrity Heartthrob Studies, UCLA.

4:30 – 5:45: 3rd session of round table discussions.

- Thespis of Icaria, 6th century BC vs. Scott Baio of Brooklyn, 1961 - ???? – Who is the greater icon?
- Scott's role as Dr. Jack Stewart on *Diagnosis Murder*: Is the character so well developed that you would rather see Scott than your usual doctor? Does watching the show make you feel healthier?
- Conspiracy Theories: Where's the Oscar? Ben Affleck has one – What's the deal? Why is Hollywood conspiring against its greatest natural talent? Are they afraid?

6:00 – 6:30: Cocktail reception.

6:45 – 8:30: Dinner, with guest speaker Willie Aames a.k.a. Buddy Lembeck from *Charles in Charge* and Peyton Nichols from

Zapped. Willie will be speaking on his role as the "sidekick", and his life before *(8 Is Enough)* and after *(Bible Man)* working with Scott Baio. How has his life been changed? The world?

8:45 - Midnight: Dance Party.

Good luck Ellen! Have a great time!

Dear Advice Savant,

I just moved in to a new neighborhood. It's a typical suburban stereotype. Rows and rows of little houses, all with fenced yards. Lots of kids riding bikes, weekend BBQs. You get the idea. My question is this; how can I get to know my new neighbors? Everyone in the neighborhood seems to be friends, and I'm having a hard time breaking in to the group.

Charlie – Bloomington, IN

Charlie,

It's never easy being the new neighbor Charlie. But there are some proven ways you can get to know your fellow suburbanites. There are three key areas to focus on:

1. You're friendly, and you want to make friends.
2. Be engaging. You're interesting and cool. You and your neighbors like the same things and have the same interests.
3. You are a valuable member of the neighborhood. You contribute something.

Be Friendly: This is the cornerstone of your strategy. Project a friendly, gracious and forthcoming personality. This will tell people that you're eager to get to know them. How to do it? Here are a couple of ideas to get you started:

- Drive around the area offering the kids free candy. What kid doesn't like candy? Or ice cream? (Note: it's hard to keep ice cream cold in your car, so it may be better to keep it at home. Just offer to bring the kids to your house.) Win over the kids, and their parents will follow. How to find the kids? Why not swing by the school just after 3:00, and see if they need a ride home? A ride with candy and ice cream that is!

- Keep your window blinds open. Appear welcoming. You're not some strange shut in who hides in his house and never talks to anyone! Keep those shades open! Spend as much time as possible standing in your front window – just staring out at the street. Make sure to wave at anyone passing by. If they don't look over, knock on the window to get their attention.

Engage: Once you've established yourself as friendly, it's time to take the initiative. Get out there Charlie! Get to know people! But do your homework first. You want to leave a good first impression. Try to learn as much about your neighbors as you can, *before* meeting them. This way, you can be prepared to talk about things they're interested in.

- Go through their garbage at night, see what you can find. You'll be amazed at what you can learn about people from what they throw away.
- Monitor their habits. Start taking notice of when they leave for work, and when they come home. Where do they work? What do they do during the day? Where do they shop? What kinds of movies do they see? Church? You'll have to follow them to find out.

- When they're gone, see how much you can learn by looking in their windows. Don't forget to take pictures to help you remember everything!

When you do finally talk with them, you should still ask questions. It's only polite. Even if you already know the answer (possibly from their garbage), you should still ask in order to be sociable. How long have they lived in the neighborhood? Do they have a family? What are all of their names? Do they have any pets? Are they gone very much? Would they like to swap house keys? Do they like the neighborhood? Do they own a gun? How are the schools? Do they need a house sitter? What day is garbage day (As if you don't already know)?

Contribute: My last bit of advice Charlie; is to make yourself a valuable member of the neighborhood. Contribute to the community. A couple of suggestions:

- Start a one man neighborhood watch. Guard your new friend's safety by "patrolling" the neighborhood at night, spending time in their yards and checking to make sure their doors are locked. Don't forget to give them a silent wave of "you're welcome" when they notice you outside their bedroom window at three-thirty in the morning. How safe they'll feel!

- Draw up a fire safety plan for each of your neighbors. This plan should have instructions on how to get out of their house, should there be a fire. Include diagrams and a detailed floor plan of their house. (Be sure to note where everyone sleeps - by name.) Stress the importance of an escape plan with phrases like "You never know when your house might burn down" or "People don't know how easy it is to start fires". They'll appreciate the consideration for their safety. (Note: Having a fire siren installed on your roof is fine, but it doesn't help anyone if it's not working. Test it regularly.)

Good luck Charlie! Enjoy your new neighborhood.

Dear Advice Savant,

I've been working part time as a substitute teacher for the local grade school. I've just been offered a 2 month job for a teacher who's out on Maternity leave. It's a great opportunity, but I'm really looking for something permanent. Should I take it?

Regis – Silverton, TX

Yes Regis,

Yes you should take the job, definitely. 2 months is a long time. At least, it's long enough for you to turn this temporary job into something permanent. You shouldn't be asking "Should I take this job". Rather, you should be asking "What am I willing to do to keep it"? Start thinking strategy Regis. And it wouldn't hurt to loosen your morals a bit. This is your career, no, your *future* we're talking about.

Phase 1: The Children

You need to win over the children. This is critical. It's not enough that they accept you; they have to forget their old teacher. Get their loyalty. How?

Tragedy: Nothing brings people together like a shared tragedy. Maybe the class turtle meets an unexpected or unfortunate end? Field trip to the planetarium cancelled? It's up to you Regis. Just remember it has to involve everyone, be there when it happens, and be supportive and sympathetic. Also (indirectly) blame it on their regular teacher for not planning ahead.

Bribe Them: Maybe a few extra minutes at recess? Or, how about artificially bumping up those grades a little bit? Failed an English quiz? Not this time, it's a "C". Being well spoken isn't that important after all, and no child needs to be taxed with bad grades. Short term fix? Sure, but the kids will love you for it. Next year it'll be some other teacher's problem to fix.

Fear: The old standby. Find an issue they all care about, and exploit it. Example: That bully on the playground could be trouble, and he's not going anywhere (already flunked 6th grade twice). Make sure the kids know (as their teacher) you'll protect them during recess. You're tough on bullies. Would their regular teacher be? Maybe (not sure), but kids - is it worth risking your lunch money?

Public Relations: Identify a few kids in the class that seem to like you. Maybe kids who didn't get along with the last teacher? Bad grades? Whatever Regis - as long as they like you, and want you as their teacher. Encourage them to start a class newspaper. Approve the stories.

Headline: *Bully kept at bay by brave new teacher. Lunch money safe. Bully still seen as potential danger in future.*

Phase 2: The Other Teachers

Winning over the class is critical, but you may still face a challenge from the other teachers. Here's how to keep them from ruining your agenda of becoming a full time teacher:

Create an issue: Teachers aren't going to be as concerned about the bully on the playground, so "Bully Fear" won't work and you'll need to find another issue (or create one) that you can leverage for support. The idea here Regis, is to connect yourself with an issue, or take a position that the other teachers can't possibly disagree with. Example: Protecting children from the evils of modern media. Movie and television violence, maybe bad language in magazines, or internet porn, etc. You get the idea. Children need their school to prepare and protect them from these "Media Dangers". Your position Regis: Lessons need to be added to the class curriculum. Lessons to save the students. Children need protection. Make sure to note (a few times) that this should have been done by their previous / regular teacher. And don't forget to insinuate that you're doing a better job than she did. *Here's the key:* If another teacher objects, you can openly accuse them of not caring about the children's safety. Be vocal. They may not be scared of the bully, but they'll be scared of being branded a "Child Hater", and they'll be scared of you. Hopefully, they'll be scared enough to remain quiet when you push for permanent placement in the school. (Note: Don't be shy about suggesting stories about "Child Hater" teachers - who oppose you - to your student "press".)

Dear Advice Savant,

I'm the regional manager for a national software company. I basically run the local branch, which is made up of software engineers, and a couple of sales staff. We've only got 8 people in our office, not including myself, so it's a pretty small group. The problem is; we're not really a team. Everyone is congenial, and respectful, but somehow detached. I'm not saying we all need to be best friends, but I would like to see the group connect a little more. With only 8 people, I would expect everyone to be closer, but they're not. I've already tried the usual "team building" activities; camp retreats, coaches, seminars, workshops, you name it. Nothing seems to do the trick. What can I do?

Philip – Scott City, KS

Philip,

You're a victim of the times. A generation ago, people cared about their place of work. A person worked for a company (the *same* company) for 30, 40, even 50 years, until they retired or their job was shipped overseas. That was the norm. Back then, the people you worked with were more than just coworkers, they were friends. They were family. You succeeded or failed together, as a company, and as a team. The long term, the big picture and the *team* was what mattered. Today's job jumpers just don't buy in to that philosophy. Six months here, six months there, "I'm a contract employee." A "Contract Employee"!? It's crazy Philip.

In today's world, people aren't receptive to coaches, seminars or team building workshops, because they just don't care. "Why should I worry about being a better team player, if I'll be on a different team next year?" Athletes are singled out and criticized for this type of thinking, but it really permeates all occupations, not just sports.

So what to do Philip? How do you get people to work together as a team? Get them to bond as a cohesive group (Especially if they don't want to)? You can't appeal to their sense of loyalty, because they have none. You can't make them *want* to be a team, because they don't want to. You need to hit them on an emotional level.

Fear.

Bypass the brain, and go straight to the gut. Place the group in a scary situation, which causes everyone to be afraid. When faced with terror, they will begin to work as a group, act as a team. The "pack" instinct will take over.

A few simple ideas:

Trapped in the Elevator
Cost: Low (Tip the building facilities team a few bucks to shut off the power.)
Difficulty Level: Easy (Still need a way to get all eight in the elevator at one time.)
Time Commitment: 6 – 7 Hours
Suggestion: Get all of them in to the elevator at once, by setting off the fire alarm. This will also add to the overall panic. Smoke bombs are a plus.
Risk: Actual fire.

Viral Outbreak – Office Quarantine

Cost: Low (Some plastic and yellow tape for the doors, plus the monkey rental fee.)

Difficulty Level: Easy

Time Commitment: 48 – 60 Hours

Suggestion: Have someone (outside the office) seal the doors with "quarantine" tape and plastic, *then* let the monkey with the bio hazard tag collar run loose through the office.

Risk: Someone may already have a cold or the flu or something and everyone could catch it.

Trapped on a Deserted Island

Cost: High

Difficulty Level: (Extremely) Difficult

Time Commitment: 6 – 7 Weeks.

Suggestion: Make sure you have them sign a release, and film the whole exercise. Then you can sell it later as a reality series.

Risk(s): They could miss the point, and indict you (kidnapping?). Also, one of the weaker office members could be eaten if the group starts to run short of food.

A few other quick (and terrifying) ideas Philip:

- Night in the Haunted Mansion
- Hostage Situation
- All-Day Pass on the "It's a Small World" ride at Disney World.
- Runaway Train
- Lunch at White Castle
- Tour of the Fox "News" Studio
- Avalanche Covered Cabin Retreat
- Rosie Perez Film Festival
- Minnesota Vikings Season Tickets

Good luck Philip!

Dear Advice Savant,

I run a consulting firm out of my home office. Business has been great. But lately, I feel like I'm starting to lose track of everything, my desk is a mess, and there are files and papers everywhere. I'm having trouble keeping track of appointments. Can you give me some advice on how to become more organized?

Dewey – Newark, NJ

Dewey,

You've definitely come to the right place.
I don't mean to "toot my own" horn here, but I may well be the most organized person in the whole world. I have been my entire life. My Lego blocks were itemized and cataloged based on color, size and quantity. When other kids were reading comic books, I was transferring them to microfiche (for easier storage and referencing). My socks are arranged by color, then frequency of use, then warmth. I haven't lost my keys in 23 years. I haven't lost anything in 20, including my temper. (Note: My emotions are also very well organized.)

Right now, my personal style of the "to do" list, is considered so efficient and effective that it's used officially by 16 international governments, on four continents, and the Vatican. NASA sends their pre-launch check lists to me for proof reading.

I'm also on the verge of completely reinventing library science, with a breakthrough system capable of organizing up to 3 million books, entirely by their smell. I guess what I'm saying here Dewey, is that you've come to someone who nose what their talking about.

But, we're not here to talk about how organized I am. We're here to talk about what a disorganized mess you are. How do you change? How do you become more like me? Becoming organized is a lifestyle. It's not something you just do, it's something you *become*. It's something that's way too big to cover in one short column. So in the interest of limited space, let's focus in the one critical need for your home office: An effective filing system.

The Filing System: Cornerstone of an organized office. *But how to create one?* First, forget the traditional methods. Color coding? Alphabetizing? What's so inherently organized about colors or the alphabet? It's outdated, unintuitive and stupid Dewey. First graders spend their time working with colors and the alphabet, look how messy they are. Here are a few more advanced ideas to get you started:

Natural Selection: Works for Mother Nature. Basically, the concept is that the strongest files survive. Healthier, more important (or dominant) clients are filed to the front, getting more attention. The clients who are smaller (and weaker) are filed in the back, getting less attention and eventually dying off. One simple method to put this system in place; is to use your key contact as a measuring point for the client companies. Between any two of them, who is stronger? Who would win in a fight for food, or stand a better chance of mating? They get bumped to the front. This will eventually improve the quality of your overall client base, by weeding out the lesser customers.

Break out of the Cabinet: Why put all of your files together? It makes no sense. Instead store your records in a more appropriate place relative to what, or who, they represent. Let's say you're doing consulting work for a bakery? - Notes in the oven. Auto Mechanic? - Filed in the garage or maybe under the hood of your car. Landscaping company? – In the yard. Republican Party? – Right in the toilet. With this method of association, you'll have no trouble remembering where you're all important customer records are. (Note: Work done for a file cabinet company should still be stored in the file cabinet.)

Don't be Confined to Paper: It's plain, flat, easy to lose and highly flammable. Why are people so quick to use it? Think about it; you have a very important document, and it's on paper. Why would you put it on a desk with thousands of other pieces of paper, all the same size, shape and color? Crazy. It's a wonder paper users ever find anything. Next time you have some important notes; why not write them on something more unique? Something easier to locate? Like say, an umbrella, or a how about a beach ball? Just try to misplace a beach ball on your desk. If you let the air out, it will still fit in your brief case, so you can bring it with you for meetings or presentations. (Note: If you are the one giving the presentation, inflate the ball *before* getting up in front of the group. If the speech is a success, you can toss it to the audience, and they'll bounce it around like at a rock concert.)

Good luck Dewey!

Dear Advice Savant,

Last week I took my 15 year old son, Francis, shopping for a new football. High school tryouts are starting, and I wanted him to get some practice. While we were at the sporting goods store, he told me that he didn't want to play football. He wanted to take ballet lessons. He wants to go shopping for tights! What do I do?

Gary – Shelby, NC

Gary,

First off, see if you can catch up with us here in the 21st century. It'll be hard for you to hear my advice, way back there in the 1950s. You're going to have to drop your outdated attitude on masculine and feminine roles in society. Give up on your old fashion stereotype centered thinking and obsolete point of view. Try to join us in the here and now. Open your mind Gary.

Now, having said that: You've got a huge problem. Unless you want your son to go through years of torment and social isolation, you've got to fix this right away.

Try to get him back in to football, or really any sport. Basketball also works. Even baseball is alright (soccer if you're desperate). Pressure him, bribe him, whatever. Just keep him on a real sports team. High school has a very simple social structure, and it's built on the foundation of sports. There's no ballet team in high school Gary, and even if there were it wouldn't have cheerleaders. No one goes to the homecoming dance recital. No one wants to go to the prom with "ballerina boy".

I also feel that I need to mention this, "Francis"? You named your son Francis?

But back to my main point, get him on to a sports team. Any team (not the chess team, whole different problem).

What if he won't play sports? What if he insists on ballet? What are the other options?

Gary, you're going to need to consider this as a possibility. I know it's hard to hear, but it's feasible he just won't be willing to play sports. Teenagers are tricky to deal with; if you push him to hard he could rebel against you. He could start wearing tights all the time, prancing through the living room. Maybe install a whole wall of mirrors in his room with one of those leg stretch bar things. Worst case; he could run away a join some kind of weirdo ballet dance circus. Then where would you be Gary?

Better to pick the battles you can win. Try to steer him to sports, but if that's not going to happen, here are a few other options:

Martial Arts: There are some martial arts that come close to dancing; at least they look kind of similar. See if you can convince

Francis to take up one of these instead of ballet. He'll still get to "dance", but if someone hassles him, he'll be able to defend himself. Also, you can tell your buddies at poker night that he's training as a fighter, not a dancer.

Rumor: Spread a rumor in the high school that Francis *needs* to take ballet as a condition of his parole. He dances, or it's back to jail. Maybe it's part of some sort of anger management technique, maybe the judge had a twisted sense of humor, or whatever. Who cares, you just need to start the rumor, and the kids at the school will run with it. If you're lucky, he'll be branded as the "bad boy", which is even higher on the social scale than a jock.

Ship him off to Russia: For a couple of years anyway. Here's the thing; in Russia, this sort of thing is looked at completely differently. Teenage boys who take ballet are *cool*.
I know it's crazy. "Have another vodka Vladimir!" But I will tell you this; if your son comes back to high school in a couple of years, speaking Russian and dancing ballet, he will somehow be cool in America. Here's how it works:

Boy + ballet = freaky + High School Social Outcast.

Russian + Boy + Ballet = Interesting + Foreign + Attractive + Popular.

It's really all about the math Gary. A couple of Russian phrases, and Francis will have to fight off the cheerleaders.

Good luck Gary!

Dear Advice Savant,

Next week, I'm starting a new job as the Assistant Systems Administrator for a local company. It's a great job, and I'm really excited about the opportunity. The problem is that I'll be managing a team of Network Engineers, and I'm worried about gaining their respect. Not to stereotype, but Network engineers are usually kind of "geeky". I'm actually pretty cool. How can I get them to accept me?

Reggie,

Let me start out with a quick observation: The simple fact that you're even asking this question, coupled with your occupation, means that you *are in fact a geek*. You are not, in fact "cool", and are presumably far from it. I'm sorry (not really) to be the one to burst your bubble on this, but seriously Reggie. Look in the mirror man; it's time to deal with reality.

Now that that's out of the way; For the purpose of this article, or, in case anyone else might be reading this that actually *is* cool, we'll fake it. Let's pretend Reggie, that you're cool too (Key word: pretend). The question then becomes: How, as a cool person, do you learn to fit in with, and even gain the respect of - geeks? Simple:

Know the Challenge: This is a simple rule that is often overlooked. For this situation, it's especially important that you are prepared, and well informed. Geeks are shy and often timid people. They'll be wary of outsiders (especially "cool" outsiders) trying to enter their group (think "pack" or "tribe"), so be prepared for the challenge. The social environment you're trying to enter is generally closed to foreigners, so don't take it personally when you're initially rejected. Don't give up and quit! Your best bet is to take things slow. Let them gradually get used to you. Don't try to rush, (i.e.: Speak directly to someone) as this could be seen as overly aggressive. Let them become familiar with you, and eventually they'll start to communicate. When this happens, be ready!

Phase 1: Being Accepted in to the Group

To be accepted, you'll need to speak their language. Once they start to initiate communication, you'll need to make the most of it, as you may only get one shot. Conversations around the office will center on things "geek", so be prepared to participate. Here are a few key topics to be familiar with:

Slashdot.org: The on-line, nerd only, news source. Read this every day. This is mandatory. **Read this every day. Let people know, you read this every day.**

Battlestar Galactica: Know the difference between the current version and the 70's series. Be prepared to discuss the differences (a female Starbuck?), and have an opinion on the strengths and weaknesses of both. (Bonus topic: Dr. Who; Same questions for discussion.)

Bill Gates: You can love him or hate him, just know why. (Hint: Hate him.) Have a story or two ready (stolen if needed) about your own experiences with Bill and his software. Possible examples: "Windows ME: why it's bad…", or "The new Halo; Will it only run on Vista?" (Bonus topic: "Linux; Brave Underdog Operating System.")

Star Trek: I know this sounds cliché, but seriously you will really need this. You'll need a working knowledge of all the different television series and movies. Know all the characters by name, including the aliens. If possible, try to learn a few Klingon phrases (yes it's a fake language that some people actually learn). I know this is a lot, but you'll immediately lose any geek credibility if you miss a simple passing reference to the *Borg Collective, Tribbles* or the *Cochran Warp Engine*.

Phase 2: Gaining Respect

Once you've been accepted, and are communicating (talking) regularly with the geeks, you can start to work on gaining their respect. Be patient! This can also take time, but here are a few things to help you move things along:

Lifestyle: Adopt the lifestyle, and don't go halfway. Example: Stop going out on weekends. Stay home and watch the SciFi channel (Note: Dr. Who and Battlestar Galactica are both on Friday night). Maybe you could spend some time on Saturday pulling the network cable out of your walls (now that you've gone to a wireless network). The key here is to talk about it. Talk about what you *didn't* do over the weekend. A demonstrated lack of a social life, will encourage bonding, and eventually respect.
(Note: Don't try to sneak out on weekends, and then lie about it. Sooner or later you'll slip up and talk about the girl you met at the bar. Unless you can prove that she's also a loser, it will do unimaginable damage to your geek-respect chances. Don't take the chance!)

Build a Computer: No self-respecting nerd buys a computer Reggie. Computers are like hot rods to these guys. Quad-Core CPU? 64 bit? What about memory? The video card? Flux Capacitor? You'll need to have a more than decent homemade PC to get any geek respect. Build it. Talk about it. Upgrade it. Talk about it more. Your PC is a direct reflection of your "skills". Show them off.

On-Line Gaming: This is going to sound a little strange Reggie, but you will actually gain real-life respect, by becoming a pretend character, and playing a game on the internet. I know, it sounds ridiculous, but you'll have to trust me on this one. Find an on-line game you like, there's lots of choices. Become "virtual tough", "virtual smart", "virtual heroic" and "virtual cool". You'll gain real-life acceptance in the nerd herd, and be rejected by (attractive) real-life women.

Kapla Reggie!

Dear Advice Savant,

I've always enjoyed writing short stories, just as a hobby. This winter, I decided to take a creative writing class at the local college, see if I could improve my writing, and maybe learn some new skills. The class is fun, but I can't seem to get anything down on paper. My final story is due in a few weeks, and except for a bad case of writers block, I've got nothing! What do I do?

Todd – Durham, NC

Having some trouble with the old "White Bull" are we Todd? I feel your pain. In addition to writing this advice column (gotta pay the bills), I'm also a devoted creative writer myself. I have a whole series of action filled short stories, centering on the adventures of Dirk Fighterjetstein. He's a gritty, retired Navy SEAL demolition expert, who wanders the country searching for his lost daughter while solving crimes and helping innocent people along the way. Catch phrase: "Blow it up!" But I'm getting off track here Todd. We're talking about writers block, and how to get past it.

Whenever I start writing a new Dirk Fighterjetstein story, I usually find myself staring helplessly down at a blank sheet of paper, or peering in to the endless abyss of the monitor's empty, haunting glow. Feeling helpless - unable to find the words. There are few things as frustrating or daunting.
Writers have been dealing with this for years, its broken braver people than we Todd.

I guess the only real advice I can offer you, is what I do to deal with it.

This is a technique I've been developing for years. It's been very helpful for me to.

1. Deal with my fear and frustration.
2. Stimulate the creative process.

The first thing I do, is have the local party shop deliver one of my specially made "writer's piñatas". These are custom made to resemble something that I personally find confusing, terrifying or frustrating. Shaped to look like something that not only makes me afraid, but also mad.

A few examples of my "writer's piñata's":

- My old high school bully.
- A clown.
- Celine Dion
- A ventriloquist dummy.
- Anne Coulter.

After an hour or so of quiet meditation, focusing my emotions, I pick up my stick (or "imagination lever") and start the artistic process. Beating the piñata allows me to work through my fear and intimidation about the work. Usually, I start off swinging slowly, almost hesitantly. Gradually, as I grow less afraid and more confident, I swing more heavily and aggressively. Eventually

working my way up to an enraged display of controlled (?) violence.
(Note: It's usually a good idea to do this indoors, where people aren't able to watch. Naïve people might not understand the delicate process of the artist, and judge you unfairly.)

There is usually some yelling toward the end, and sometimes tears.
(Another note: Clear this with your neighbors first. I've had the cops called on me a few times.)

Once the piñata is broken (smashed), I begin to organize my thoughts.
Here's the trick, instead of candy, I fill my piñatas full of small domino-sized chips, each with a different word on them. (Also, some candy, to keep me interested.) I arrange the words in to sentences, as closely as possible to the way they've landed on the floor.
An example: Let's say I'm writing one of my stories, and I just can't get the next chapter started. After I've destroyed my Donald Rumsfeld piñata, I'll use the fallen word chips to help me get going. Let's say the chips spelled out: Suitcase – Elephant – Banana – Window – Car – Hat.

This would translate into:

- Dirk packed his *suitcase* while nursing an *elephant* sized hangover. *Banana* daiquiris were his favorite drink, but he'd never let his old Navy buddies know. He glanced out the *window* to see a *car* coming up the drive. His cab, coming to take him to the airport. He closed his suitcase, put on his *hat*, and walked out the door.

See Todd, it's like the stories just write themselves.

Good luck Todd!
Blow it up!

Dear Advice Savant,

Recently, I found I'd been gaining weight. Now, I've always worked out several times a week, and tried to eat well. There's no real history of obesity in my family. So, the weight gain seemed strange to me. Not being able to explain it, I visited my doctor; only to find out I have a small woman sticking out from under my left shoulder blade. Is this normal? How does something like this happen? What do I do?

Chester – Biloxi, MS

First off Chester: Remain calm.

She's probably just as scared as you are, and we don't want anyone to panic here. Try not to make the situation worse by losing your cool. This kind of thing happens more often than you might think. In fact, it happened to me just last spring.

I was getting one of those massages where they walk barefoot on your back. Everything was fine, until the woman stepped in the wrong place and "whoosh" - sank down right between two of my ribs. Just like quicksand, right up to her neck.

It all happened so quickly; she started to struggle, and then of course, I started freaking out. And I mean FREAKING OUT! (Note: Here again Chester, let me remind you of the importance of staying calm.) Next thing you know I'm out of there, running down the street in nothing but a towel, with this woman's screaming head coming out of my back. I'm waving my arms, yelling for help, pointing at my back. People are scattering everywhere, children are crying, you get the idea.

Not a pretty scene. And it's never fun to spend the night in detox. Looking back, I probably could have handled the situation better.

I'm not sure if you're a massage victim as well, or exactly how this happened to you Chester. It really doesn't matter though. The important thing now is to get her out of there, and since you're apparently calm, we can better choose how to move forward. Decide in a rational way, how to best take care of this.

Talk to her: Has she said anything? (Probably not, I'm sure you would have mentioned it.) Maybe she's in shock? In any case, see if you can communicate with her. Find out who she is. Where she's from? Be sure to speak in soothing tones. Don't get excited. You don't want her to become alarmed and start moving around. Trust me, this is bad. Try to reassure her if you can. Bond with her. Tell her it's going to be all right, maybe inject some humor; "Hey, get off my back! Ha-ha-ha!" you could hum some "Baby got back", etc. Connect with her. You're both in this together; try to have each other's back.

Keep her as comfortable as possible: Start using stools, stay away from chairs, especially wicker. Don't sleep on your back, and for heaven's sake don't lie down in the tub! You could drown the poor woman! No heavy coats either. No backpacks (fanny packs are cool). No sit ups. No summersaults. No break dancing.

Get medical attention: Have a friend drive you to the CER (Chiropractic Emergency Room). These people are trained to deal with emergencies just like this. Gunshot wounds, broken bones, head trauma, etc, the best place to be when you're critically injured, is in the hands of a chiropractor. The highly trained teams of the CER are the best in the business. These brave men and women can re-align miracles. With a little luck, they may be able to adjust her out of you right on the spot.

Dear Advice Savant,

I'm 38 and I can't seem to find a girlfriend. To be honest, I've never really had that much luck with the ladies. I've done a lot of thinking, and decided that the best way for me to change my luck, is to get super powers, and fight crime. How can I get super powers?

Ronny – Warren, PA

Wow Ronny,

You put me in kind of a tough place here. Normally, my advice for someone in your position would be to recommend one of two things:

1. Accept how pathetic you are, and hurry up getting used to being alone.

   \- Or -

2. Quit your job at the comic book store, move out of your parents' basement, and get a life.

But no, not this time. Something about you seems different Ronny. I'm going to give you the benefit of the doubt. I'm going to assume that you're (somewhat) normal, living on your own. That you have a career. That you're somewhat attractive. That you're a normal, functioning, member of society who's based in reality. However, for some reason completely out of your control, you just can't seem to land that girlfriend. I'm going to assume that you're not just a loser Ronny, and you really do need super human powers.

So, how to get them? There are a few key ways:

Technology: While this may not technically be "powers", or "super human", I think it goes along with what you're after. The idea here is to wear some kind of super suit, or armor, which protects you and gives you super strength or speed. Maybe you have a utility belt, or array of special gadgets. Tech tools in your fight against crime. How to get them?

I'm guessing you're no genius or tech wizard who could build his own super gizmos or you would have already. And would therefore be rich, and would therefore already have lots of girlfriends.

Instead, my advice would be to seek out the help of someone with means. A sponsor, who's got the money, and know how to equip you, build your super gadgets, or tailor your special suit. I'd recommend forming a partnership with the *Ronco* Guy. Not only is he able to produce lots of crap, but he's clearly insane. Perfect match for you Ronny.

Freak Accident: Usually this would happen in some sort of secret lab, or government project. Think: Exposure to some kind of unusual radioactivity? Or, maybe a mishap involving the ingestion of a secret "formula"? You get the idea. The point here is you need to be in the right place, at the right time. Try to get a job working in a lab. If you can, try to hook up with a (mad) scientist, or better yet a chemist who's recently been released from jail for his "questionable theories and practices." The upside: easy access to experimental, possibly illegal, situations. The downside: A lack of control over what your powers would be.

With the tech gear, you know exactly what will happen. In a freak accident, you're never really sure what you'll get. It could backfire. While it could be nice to be able to run really fast, walk through walls, turn invisible, etc. You could also end up with "Super Laziness", "Incredible Gas" or "Amazing Sweatiness". To this point, stay away from secret formulas that involve fiber.

(Note: Something like "Incredible Dancing" wouldn't do much for the crime fighting, but may help with the ladies, so I guess it's kind of a wash.)

Somehow be an alien: Aliens always seem to have powers. Some aliens are really super. They can fly, run fast, stop bullets, see through stuff, etc. etc. Other extra terrestrials can only heal fingers, or "ouches". In any case, they all seem to be able to do something. So Ronny, while it's probably unlikely that you're an alien, it wouldn't hurt to check before trying anything else. If you do happen to be an alien, it's great because there's really nothing else to do: No effort, easy super powers. Plus, it only takes a minute to run upstairs and ask your parents.

Good luck Ronnie!

Dear Advice Savant,

This fall, I'm traveling to Germany with a group of friends from high school. It'll be my first trip there, or anywhere outside the US. I'm excited, but a little nervous. I don't even speak the language. Can I get some first time traveler advice?

Jeremy – Wausau, WI

Jeremy,

Travel is one of the best ways to learn and grow as an individual. Being able to experience other cultures and societies will teach you things you could never learn in school. Discovering the world teaches us new ideas and about tolerance of other cultures, while also forcing you to examine your own. Travel provides invaluable life lessons. Especially if you're from Wisconsin.

The essential element, or "key", to getting the most out of your trip is to immerse yourself as much as possible; in to the society you are visiting. Try to *be* German. Think like a German. Act like a German.

This starts at home, weeks before boarding the plane. The question then becomes: How does one *become* German, having never been to Germany? How do you begin?

Stereotypes: Being politically correct went out with the 90's. In this new golden age of the "with us or against us" attitude, you're free to fully embrace the German stereotype as much as you like. Use this to your advantage, while preparing for your trip.

Stop bathing every day: Try skipping that shower once in a while. (What are you, Royalty?) See if you can work your way up to one bath a week. Give yourself some time for this. Set goals – Dirty Goals. Also, you might want to stop washing your clothes so much. Socks are good for 3 or 4 days. Make sure you're getting the full use out of your wardrobe between every wash. Benchmark tip: If someone, say on a bus or something, happens to make an off-hand comment about you or your clothes, then you know you're ready. *Note: This only applies to comments related to lack of washing: visible dirt, unpleasant scent, etc. Any other comments about you and your clothes (i.e. sense of style) don't count.*

Play the German: Remember, as far as you're concerned, you're German. Or at least you're trying to be. Try to embrace a German frame of mind, and approach conversations from this perspective.

When meeting someone, or having a dialog, some examples of useful comments might be:
"I really do enjoy beer and bratwurst. They are certainly delicious. I also like kraut."
"Which way is Poland?"

"My lederhosen tend to chafe when doing the polka."
"David Hasselhoff's musical artistry has gone largely unappreciated in the west."

Which brings me to my next point:

Germans Love David Hasselhoff: This point cannot be stressed enough. Yes, everyone worldwide loves David Hasselhoff, this is not in question. The Germans however, love his *music.* You too, must therefore show love for his music. Exude it. Concert t-shirt? Fine, but not good enough. You want everyone in the room to know that you're listening to him. The problem with portable music players (i-pods, and so on), is that no one knows what you're listening to. If you can find one, use an older - shoulder mounted "boom-box", and play it loud. If you must use an i-pod, just make sure to sing along so everyone can hear.

Learning the Language: It's a common misconception that learning the native language of the country you're visiting will make the trip easier and more fulfilling. This couldn't be more wrong. Don't spend your valuable pre-trip prep time in front of an old text book, trying to conjugate German verbs. It's worthless.

You'll really only need to learn one or two phrases, and how to use them effectively.
Example: "Can you help me find a restaurant?" (A common phrase, and very practical.)
Practice using this phrase while looking a little frustrated. Repeat the phrase quietly, several times. Furrow your brow.
With a little luck, people will think you're actually German, but just stupid. They'll be nicer to you, and may even personally show you the way to the restaurant.

Alles Gute Jeremy!

Dear Advice Savant,

I'm trying to impress my new girlfriend. Her birthday is coming up, and I'd like to show her how much I care, but we haven't been together very long. What kind of present should I get?

Dan, Rock Springs, WY

Well Dan,

Let's first clarify what we're talking about here. This is an actual girlfriend? This isn't just a girl you know, and are maybe hoping to date one day? You've had "the talk", and you're actually dating? It's official and everything?

Honestly Dan, if you're just some freak following this woman around, I don't want to help you. Just to be clear.

So, that said, let's give you the benefit of the doubt, and get down to business. The trick when picking a birthday gift for someone special (in your case a girlfriend) is to *know* that person. What does she like? You'll make her feel special by demonstrating that you know her interests. That you really know *her*, and you've really thought about what she'd enjoy. Now, this doesn't mean you should peer in her windows, or go rooting through her garbage to find out more about her.

Seriously Dan, are you paying attention here? That's just plain wrong. Sending her a love letter is great. But not twelve letters a day. Having her picture on your desk is fine, but no one likes a guy who decorates his office with wall to wall, floor to ceiling pictures of his “girlfriend”. Especially if it’s obvious that she didn’t even know the pictures were being taken. Where did you take the pictures from Dan? Across the street? Or maybe from the bushes? Own a telephoto lens Dan? They lock people up for stuff like that.

But, assuming you’re on the up and up. The key thing to remember is spending time together. The gift is nice, but anyone can buy something. Being together is what matters most. Actually, being together *voluntarily* is what matters most. She doesn’t want to come home and find you hiding in her apartment. *Stay off her fire escape Dan!* Don’t follow her to work, or frequent her favorite coffee shop. *Stockings* can be romantic, but not *stalkings.*

You know what Dan, forget it. I don’t trust you, or your motives. For anyone else reading, just get a puppy. They’re cute, people like them. Plus, they live like 10 or 12 years. So, if they end up dumping you, they have the hassle getting rid of the dog too. Dan, get some help. Seriously, before someone gets hurt or arrested.

Dear Advice Savant,

I'm planning to buy a new town home. After looking for a few months, I've narrowed it down to a few choices, but I'm still undecided. My question is this: Should I buy a new house that's just been built, or pay a little less for a one that's older, say built in the 1970's

- Rita, Glendale, CA

Rita,

With the recent housing boom, this type of question comes up a lot. I would definitely recommend buying the newly built town home. Never consider the older one.

Yes, you'll probably pay a little more upfront, but you'll be getting a brand new house. New appliances. New plumbing. An up-to-date heating and cooling system. In many cases, the builder will even let you pick the carpet, paint, cabinets, etc. This gives you the chance to style the home you way you'd like it. Not to mention that everything is installed by professionals.

Plus, with a newly built home, there are no previous owners to worry about. Who knows what kind of disturbing, weirdo behavior has happened in a used house? Would you buy a used toothbrush? A used pair of underwear? No Rita, of course you wouldn't. It's gross.

What about animals? Did they have pets? Big pets? Maybe they raised livestock? Maybe they raised livestock and butchered it on the kitchen counter. How can you be sure? Rita, when you set your coffee down on the kitchen counter, you want to know that the only fluids (animal?) smeared on it, have come from you.

There's really no way to tell how these freaks may have spent their time in your would-be home. Disco parties? Witchcraft? Animal sacrifices? *Think Rita!* Were they in a cult? Spot any daggers lying around?

Bottom line Rita, you can't check everything. You can't boil a whole house to kill germs. (Not easily anyway) The standard home inspection doesn't check for ancient burial grounds.

(*Buyers hint: Bring a dog. They can sense things we can't, i.e. ghosts.*)

The last thing to consider is resale. Over the next several years, as the baby boomer generation retires, they'll be looking to sell their big family houses and make the move to smaller, easier to care for town homes and condos. It'll be a seller's market for you. Think about it Rita, lot's of rich, lazy retirees lining up to buy your beautiful, only *slightly* used house.

A house in which you've never, ever, killed an animal.

(*Sellers hint: Don't be afraid to list "No animal sacrifices" on the home description.*)

All I'm saying Rita, is that there's a lot more to consider when buying a 70's house than just ripping out shag carpet or trying to get rid of that musty "High Karate" smell. These houses have a history.

Sometimes a dark one.

Think Rita.

Dear Advice Savant,

I'm planning a big party next month. I'll be having people from work come, and some old college friends, maybe some neighbors. I really want my party to be fun, but I'm scared that it won't be. What can I do to make sure everyone has a good time?

Gwen – Rushville, IL

Gwen,

First off, stop over thinking it. You'll only make yourself nervous. Throwing a party should be fun, don't get so worried that you don't have a good time. First tip: RELAX! This is about fun. When you're having fun, your guests will too. In many ways, fun is like a horribly contagious flesh eating virus. It spreads quickly, and is usually airborne, although it can also be contracted through physical contact.

It sounds like they'll be a few different groups of people coming to the party. The most important thing to remember for any party is to keep people moving around and talking to one another. Get everyone engaged. People need to mingle, if they want to "catch the fun". This is the cardinal rule for any social gathering. Make sure your college friends are talking to your work friends, and vice versa. If everyone just stays in their own little "safe" groups, your party's a failure, and so are you Gwen.

How do you get people talking? Everyone knows the trick of putting food at one end of the room, and drinks at the other. I suppose it does keep people moving, but it's really pretty stupid.

Think about it, groups of silent, bored people wandering back and forth? Failure Gwen. Sad, pathetic failure.

Here are a few better ideas and activities that will keep people moving, talking, and engaged:

Let's find the smell. – This is a fun game that will keep people circulating around the house (and usually outside too). It's also a good ice breaker for starting conversations. *It's not in the garbage? Did something die?* Maybe a prize for whoever finds the smell? Maybe the smell could be one of your guests? Lots of ways to do this game. Lots of fun at your party.

Who's the angry stranger in the corner? – Talk about a conversation starter! Your guests will find it easier to talk with one another, if they're all scared of the same person. For this game, I usually try to find someone older, grizzled, and surly. (Drunk if possible, with wild mood swings and a quick temper.) Keep things exciting! (Maybe and ex-con?) It's up to you Gwen, use your imagination.
Tip: Try to find someone with Tourettes syndrome.

Quiet alone time / Reading time. – Just kidding Gwen!

Indoor obstacle course. – Who doesn't love an obstacle course? What a way to get people circulating! Weaving through the dining room chairs, around the lamp, over the back of the couch and finishing at the stove (Which incidentally, has a built in timer!). Who will win the race? Who's up to the challenge? Who knows first aid? This game is a thrill for everyone, especially later in the evening after they've had a few drinks.

One last thing to remember Gwen: No party is boring, if something's on fire.

Good Luck!

Dear Advice Savant,

My company was bought out, downsized, sold off in pieces, and finally closed its doors last month. For the first time in over 16 years, I'm looking for a new job. I have extensive work experience, but not much practice interviewing. How should I prepare myself?

Henry, Portland, OR

Henry,

Unfortunately, there are lots of people out there looking for a job these days. Often, you'll be competing for jobs against kids who are just coming out of college. Most of them will be younger, more attractive, and (let's face it) probably smarter than you.

Also, they're willing to work for less money.

Henry, you have no chance at landing a job only on your merits, personality or appeal. Your best bet is to make a lasting impression. Stand out, be unique, and be remembered.

With this in mind, here are a few key things to focus on during the interview:

Be Interested and Attentive – Make sure to show interest in what the interviewer is saying.

- Sit as close to them as you can, mere inches away if possible. Don't be afraid to lean in even closer using a quick, jerking forward motion.
- Be sure to maintain eye contact, stare straight at them through the whole conversation. Never look away or get

distracted – NEVER look away! Squint if you need to, but try not to blink. Liars blink Henry, don't look like a liar.

Show Your Communication Skills – Respond as quickly as you can.

- If possible, try to answer questions before they even finish asking. (If you interrupt, and they don't immediately stop talking, just keep speaking louder and talk over them until they shut up.)
- It also usually helps to use hand gestures. Point at them, or wave your arms around. Use a clenched fist to express sincerity and commitment to your ideals.

Note: Another key communication skill is the ability to use slang. Mix slang into the conversation whenever you can. (It wouldn't hurt to have some on your resume either.) Also: Try to combine your skills, for example: Use slang (loudly) while pointing and staring. Guaranteed recipe for success Henry.

Be Goal Oriented– Everyone wants to know you can set goals, and then meet (or exceed) them. Be ready to discuss this. They want to know you'll finish what you start. Henry, show you'll be able to execute, and complete tasks and projects. Try to talk about specific things you've completed in the past like "Probation", or "Drug Rehab" (twice).

Show You're a Team Player – How you work in groups is extremely important. Employers are looking for someone who can pull people together and work within a team. "Someone who facilitates cooperation". Be sure to talk about your teamwork experience (i.e. you've worked within groups).

- Discuss your participation and manipulation tactics. How you've created "rifts".
- Mention your ability to control weaker members, and how you've eliminated competition. *(Be specific Henry!)*

Here again, use real life examples like "My anger management group", or "The gun club".
Hint: Try to bring out the positive. For example: Instead of just talking about anger management, approach it from the perspective "How my temper has helped me succeed".

Creativity and Problem Solving – Show how creative you can be! Problem solving is a must for any job. Being creative and having the ability to contribute new ideas will give you an edge on the competition. Example: Don't just say: "I burned it down for revenge". Instead, talk about the creative and original ways you came up with to make the fire look like an accident. Interview gold Henry!

Lastly – Your answers are important! You've only got one chance to convince them you're the right person for the job! If you don't feel they're impressed by an answer you've given, stop talking immediately!

- Raise your hands in the air.
- Wave them around *(hand gestures)*.
- Yell *"Woa! Do Over! My Bad!"*

Then answer again. Change your response to something they'll like more.

Good luck Henry!

www.advicesavant.com

Get some advice.

www.ingramcontent.com/pod-product-compliance
Ingram Content Group UK Ltd.
Pitfield, Milton Keynes, MK11 3LW, UK
UKHW041937190726
13854UKWH00004B/1638

9 780615 184180